REACHING OUR WORLD

KEN ADAMS

REACHING
OUR WORLD

IMPACT

ImpactDisciples.com

BEFORE YOU BEGIN.......

Right before Jesus left this planet, He told His disciples, "But you will receive power when the Holy Spirit has come upon you, and you will be My witnesses in Jerusalem and in all Judea and Samaria, and to the ends of the earth." If we take these words seriously, then we must be committed to reaching our world!

If we are going to be successful in reaching our world for Jesus, we need to know how to do what Jesus did. We need to have a clear understanding of how we reach our Jerusalem, our Judea and Samaria, and our ends of the earth. In the same way the first disciples followed Jesus' pattern to reach their world, we should follow his pattern to reach our world.

Reaching Our World is a course designed to help you understand how to obey what Christ said in Acts 1:8. As you work through these weekly lessons remember that the truths discovered in these lessons will serve as a guide for how to reach the world for Christ. The biblical principles you will learn in this course will be a foundation for understanding the direction and course of your life. You will want these principles to become a lifestyle you live out daily.

In order to lay a solid foundation, I would like to recommend a few things. *First*, give your best to each lesson. Don't rush through the lessons and skim the reading. Give it your best effort and look up all the verses so that you know what God is saying. *Second*, commit yourself to the daily scripture reading. The scripture reading is designed to supplement the lesson and using the acrostic A.C.T.S. will help God's word come alive to you every day. *Third*, commit yourself to the weekly memory verse. Memorizing scripture is one of the most important things you can do to grow spiritually so give this discipline your best effort. *Fourth*, be present at the group meetings. Anyone can do the lessons on his or her own but you can't discuss what you are learning on your own. The group time is a valuable aspect of your spiritual growth process.

Over the next few weeks, I pray that you will discover the purpose of your life and I pray that these life essentials will be true of you for a lifetime.

Being and Building Disciples,

Ken Adams

WEEK ONE: INTRODUCTION TO REACHING OUR WORLD

Goal: Understanding God's Plan to Reach Our World

Have you ever wondered if Christians could ever really reach the world for Jesus Christ? Most Christians know that Christ has called us to reach the world but we don't really believe we can or we just don't know how. If Christ does intend for us to reach the world, then surely He would give us a plan that would make it possible? One of the greatest challenges we face is discovering what that plan is and being committed to working the plan Christ has given us!

A PLAN THAT WORKS!

Two thousand years ago Christ gave His Church the power and the plan to reach the world. We still have the power and if we work the plan He gave us, the plan will work. Christ's power and plan to reach the world is clearly stated in the Book of Acts. Not long after Jesus had risen from the dead, He came to His disciples and He instructed them to reach the world! What did Jesus say in Acts 1:8? _____

_____

_____

_____

_____

Being Christ's witnesses in Jerusalem, Judea, Samaria, and the ends of the earth pretty well encompasses reaching the entire world. It means the same thing as the phrase "all nations" found in Matthew 28:19. Why did Jesus instruct us to make disciples of all nations?

_____

_____

_____

MEMORY VERSE

Acts 1:8

WEEKLY BIBLE READING

Read the passage and write out an insight on at least one of the following:

A: Attitude to change
C: Command to obey
T: Truth to believe
S: Sin to confess

☐ **MONDAY**
Psalm 105:1-6

1

BEING WITNESSES

When Jesus told His disciples to *"be my witnesses"*, He wanted them to begin in Jerusalem with the people they knew. He then expected them to go into Judea and Samaria and extend their witness geographically and culturally. Finally, Jesus wanted the disciples to go far beyond their comfort zone and reach people at what they considered to be the ends of the earth. Christ's plan was really very simple. Start reaching the people closest to you and then keep expanding your reach until you get to the ends of the earth.

START IN JERUSALEM

Christ's plan to reach the world started when the Christians living in Jerusalem reached out to their family, friends, and neighbors. What was taking place in Acts 2:47? _____

_____

_____

Where did the people being saved everyday come from?

_____

_____

How were the believers in Jerusalem described in Acts 5:42? _____

_____

_____

Being witnesses in Jerusalem is what we might call "personal or relational" evangelism. We begin reaching our world by reaching the people we already know! Personal or relational evangelism is simply living a lifestyle of identifying, praying for, connecting with, and sharing Christ with people who are far from God. Imagine what would happen if everyone in our church was committed to living a lifestyle of personal evangelism?

☐ **THURSDAY**
Ezekiel 3:16-21

MOVE TO JUDEA AND SAMARIA

Christ wanted the message of His resurrection to extend beyond the geographical and cultural borders of Jerusalem. He wanted the message of forgiveness and salvation to extend past Jerusalem into Judea and Samaria. What did God have to do to get the message into Judea and Samaria according to Acts 8:1? _____

_____
_____
_____

How was Philip's witness described in Acts 8:5, 6? _____
_____
_____

☐ **FRIDAY**
Isaiah 12:1-6

_____

How does Acts 9:31 describe the spread of the Gospel into Judea and Samaria? _____
_____
_____

Being witnesses in Judea and Samaria might be considered "local or corporate" evangelism. As we start reaching the people we know, we then begin to expand our reach into other geographical, racial, economic, and social territories. Typically, the church works together rather than alone to expand to these types of areas. Imagine what could happen if a church were identifying, praying for, connecting with, and sharing Christ corporately to local areas that went beyond friends and family?

GO TO THE ENDS OF THE EARTH

Christ clearly instructed His disciples to take his message past Jerusalem, past Judea and Samaria and take it to the farthest places they knew where people lived. Where were Barnabas and Paul (also called Saul) when the Holy Spirit called them for the first missionary journey? _____ _____(Acts 13:1). What were they doing when the Holy Spirit called them to go? _____ How did Paul describe his missionary efforts in Romans 15:19? _____ _____ _____

What was Paul's goal according to verse 20?_____ _____ _____

Being a witness to the ends of the earth might be referred to as "global or world-wide" evangelism. The goal of global evangelism is to make it possible for every person, in every nation, in every generation to have a chance to be a disciple of Jesus Christ. Every person might not be able to go to the ends of the earth but every person can help get the message there. Imagine what might happen if everyone in a church were identifying, praying for, giving, or going to distant lands to share the Gospel?

WORKING THE PLAN

Christ's plan will work if we will work His plan! So, let's get very practical for a minute. If you and every person in this church were committed to working the plan of personal, local or corporate, and global outreach, imagine how honored God would be by that. So what would such a plan look like?

First, we must regularly teach "Reaching Our World" principles.

If every small group worked through this booklet every year and we had classes on Reaching Our World, it would soon create an evangelistic culture within our church.

Second, we must provide "Reaching Our World" opportunities.

If every small group talked weekly about the opportunities in our church to invite friends, get involved in local missions, and support global missions, think how much could be done for Christ.

Third, we need a "Reaching Our World" champion in every group.

If each small group in our church had a volunteer that made "Reaching Our World" opportunities a priority in their group, that would take our evangelism efforts to a new level.

INDIVIDUAL ACCOUNTABILITY

With this booklet you will receive a "30 Day Accountability Guide" (page 32) for Reaching Our World. In the upcoming lessons, we will give a more in-depth explanation of the card but if you used this type of card every month for a year, imagine how much more focused you would be on Reaching Our World. If nothing else, regularly thinking about your Jerusalem, Judea and Samaria, and the ends of the earth will move you forward in becoming an Acts 1:8 disciple.

God has called us to "Reach Our World" and we are committed to answering that call. As individuals and a church, we have a plan to be intentional about personal, local, and global evangelism. God will do His part and our job is to do ours. We have a plan to reach our world and we have the power to reach our world. All we need now is the willingness to work the plan. I pray that this booklet will simply be a catalyst to a new lifestyle for you. I pray that you will live a lifestyle that is focused on reaching your Jerusalem, Judea and Samaria and the ends of the earth.

QUESTIONS FOR GROUP DISCUSSION OR PERSONAL REFLECTION

➤ How do you think most Christians and churches are doing at reaching our world these days?

➤ Read Acts 1:8. What does this verse tell us about God's heart for the world and our part in helping to reach it for Christ?

➤ If you were describing your "Jerusalem", how would you describe your commitment to sharing Christ with the people you know?

➤ Today, reaching your Judea and Samaria looks different unless you live in Israel. What does this look like for us today?

➤ How well is your church organized to reach the local community and how involved are you in those outreach efforts?

➤ How could every believer, everywhere, be a part of reaching the ends of the earth for Christ?

➤ Evaluate your global evangelism efforts on a scale of 1 to 10 with 10 being very committed and explain your answer.

➤ What are your thoughts about the "Reaching Our World" plan and what would help it to succeed?

➤ Would you be willing to serve as a "Reaching Our World" champion for our small group?

➤ Take a minute and pray for each other as you begin this new course.

WEEK TWO: COMMITTED TO PERSONAL EVANGELISM

Goal: Understanding How to Reach Your Jerusalem

Reaching our world begins by reaching out to the people you already know. That means intentionally sharing Christ with the people in your Jerusalem. Family members, friends, neighbors, and associates would represent your Jerusalem. You are part of God's plan to reach the world. Your commitment to live a lifestyle of identifying, praying for, caring for, and sharing with people you know that are far from God is a big step in reaching our world. How would you evaluate your current commitment and efforts in personal evangelism? _____

_____

_____

_____

STEPS FOR REACHING YOUR JERUSALEM

Reaching your Jerusalem begins with the understanding that God can use you to bring people to faith in Christ. You must realize that leading people to faith in Christ is not just something pastors do. It is the job and calling of every single disciple. What was one of the first things Jesus told his original disciples when he called them in Matthew 4:19?_____

_____

_____

STEP ONE: IDENTIFY RECEPTIVE PEOPLE

The very first step in reaching your Jerusalem is simply identifying the people in your life that are far from God and those who are receptive to the message of Christianity. This is exactly what Jesus did. Jesus looked for people who were receptive to his message everywhere he went.

MEMORY VERSE

Proverbs 11:30

WEEKLY BIBLE READING

Read the passage and write out an insight on at least one of the following:

A: Attitude to change
C: Command to obey
T: Truth to believe
S: Sin to confess

☐ **MONDAY**
Romans 1:15-17

How is this principle of receptivity demonstrated in the encounter between Jesus and Zacchaeus in Luke 19:1-9?

_____

_____

_____

_____

☐ **TUESDAY**
1 Peter 3:13-17

Jesus identified Zacchaeus as a seeker and with a simple invitation Jesus discovered he was receptive to learning more about what He had to offer him.

Identifying receptive people begins with thinking about the places you go where you might meet people far from God and then thinking about the people you meet in those places that are far from God and possibly receptive to him. Take a minute and write down three places you frequent where you could meet lost people.

_____

_____

_____

Now, take a minute and write down the names of three people you know that might be far from God but possibly receptive to knowing more about him.

☐ **WEDNESDAY**
1 Corinthians
15:1-11

_____

_____

_____

If you have a heart for reaching our world, you will learn to live a lifestyle of regularly identifying people in your life that are far from God and looking to give them an invitation to discover more.

STEP TWO: PRAY FOR OPEN DOORS

The second step in reaching your Jerusalem is to pray and ask God to open doors to connect with people far from God. What did Paul ask the Colossians to pray for in Colossians 4:3? _____

_____

_____

_____

When you have identified people who need Christ and then pray for God to give you opportunities to connect with them, He will often open doors for you to connect with them.

What can we pray for according to the following verses?

John 16:8: _____

2 Timothy 2:26: _____

John 6:44: _____

2 Corinthians 4:4 _____

☐ **THURSDAY**
Philemon
1:4-7

STEP THREE: CONNECT RELATIONALLY

The third step in reaching your personal Jerusalem is to connect relationally with the people to which God has opened the door. Typically, more people come to faith in Christ through a family member or a friend than any other way. Clearly, God uses relationships to build bridges between believers and non-believers. The best way to build a relationship for sharing Christ is to meet a need for someone or spend time talking with them.

Needs come in many different ways. Needs may be physical, emotional, social or spiritual. List some examples of the needs people in your life may have that could be opportunities to connect with them.

☐ **FRIDAY**
Acts 20:17-25

_____

_____

_____

_____

Starting a conversation with someone about Christ is easier than you might think. Here is a little tool to help you begin a conversation with someone and get to know him or her better.

"F.I.R.E"

F: Ask them about their family
I: Talk to them about their interests
R: Ask them about their religious background or church
E: Share your experience with Christ

9

STEP FOUR: SHARE THE MESSAGE OF CHRIST

**PRAYER
REQUESTS**

The fourth step in reaching your Jerusalem is sharing Christ with the people you have connected with relationally. The fear associated with sharing Christ with people is the reason why so many people never share the message of Christ with others. The Holy Spirit can give you the power to overcome those fears and give you confidence in sharing the message of Christ. What does Jesus tell us in John 15:26, 27?_____

_____

_____

_____

As the Holy Spirit empowers you, there are some simple things you can do to present the message of Christ to others. Here are a few suggestions for how to present the gospel to others.

Share your personal testimony!

Nothing is more powerful than sharing one's personal experience with Christ. People can argue with many things regarding Christ but they can't argue with your own personal experience. Your personal testimony involves three things. It involves sharing how your life was before meeting Christ, how you met Christ, and how your life has changed since meeting Christ. What did the blind man who had been healed by Jesus say in John 9:25? _____

_____

Memorize and share the gospel with your hand!

The gospel in your hand is a simple tool to help you memorize some of the basics of the gospel. With each finger, you will memorize a principle and a verse. Having this as a resource will help you explain to others the simple message of Christ.

Know the Roman Road!

The Roman Road is another tool that can be used to help you share the message of Christ with others. The Roman Road is a handful of verses taken from the Book of Romans that explains the gospel in a clear and simple manner. Take a minute and look up these verses in the "Roman Road" and mark them in your Bible or commit them to memory.

Romans 3:23, "for all have sinned and fall short of the glory of God"

Romans 5:8, "but God shows his love for us in that while we were still sinners, Christ died for us."

Romans 6:23, "For the wages of sin is death, but the free gift of God is eternal life in Christ Jesus our Lord."

Romans 10:9-10, "if you confess with your mouth that Jesus is Lord and believe in your heart that God raised him from the dead, you will be saved. For with the heart one believes and is justified, and with the mouth one confesses and is saved."

Romans 10:13, "For everyone who calls on the name of the Lord will be saved."

Give a gospel tract to someone and discuss it!

There is no shortage of printed material to use in sharing the gospel with someone. The key, however, in personal evangelism is to make it personal. In other words, let the printed material or tract be used as a tool to initiate a personal conversation. Write a quick summary of what happened with Philip in Acts 8:27-31. _____

_____

_____

_____

_____

Ask your group leader which types of materials he or she recommends in sharing their faith.

Invite to an evangelistic event!

One of the best ways to share Christ is to extend and invitation to someone you have connected with to attend an evangelistic event or service. Most churches plan events from time to time where the gospel message will be clearly explained and shared. Always use these kinds of events to jump start personal conversations about Christ. Allow the event to be an opportunity to talk about what was said or communicated and what the person thought about it.

Use resources to help you share!

Christians today have an incredible amount of resources available to help them share the message of Christ. The Internet has given us a vast amount of websites filled with helpful resources to help share the gospel. Listed below are a number of recommended sites you can use to help you share Christ with others.

GotQuestions.org

Truelife.org

Equip.org

Bible.org

Carm.org

30 DAY ACCOUNTABILITY GUIDE

Section 1

Name:_____ / **30 DAY ACCOUNTABILITY GUIDE** / Month:_____

COMMIT-MENTS	RECOGNIZE	PRAYER	ACTION
PERSONAL OUTREACH	Person or Place for Outreach 1._____ 2._____ 3._____	Personal Prayer Focus ☐ Week One ☐ Week Two ☐ Week Three ☐ Week Four	☐ Invite ☐ Care / Serve ☐ Share

QUESTIONS FOR GROUP DISCUSSION OR PERSONAL REFLECTION

➤ Which word best describes your current level of personal evangelism? (Pretty Strong, Hit or Miss, Very Weak)

➤ Take a minute and look at the Reaching Our World 30 Day Accountability Guide and share a few names that would be part of your personal Jerusalem.

➤ What places do you frequent where you are likely to meet lost people?

➤ How would you describe your prayer life for people that are far from God? Name an unbeliever that you are currently and consistently praying for?

➤ Have you ever led anyone to Christ? Explain how that happened.

➤ What does it look like when you intentionally care for someone that is not a believer? Give some examples of how you could do this for someone.

➤ Talk through the acrostic F.I.R.E and explain when and where you might be able to use it.

➤ Take some time and share the Gospel in Your Hand or the Roman Road with the rest of your group. Do it from memory!

➤ Spend some time praying that God would give you opportunities to connect with people far from God open doors share Christ with them.

WEEK THREE: COMMITTED TO CORPORATE EVANGELISM

Goal: Understand How to Reach Your Judea and Samaria

The spread of the gospel in the first century began in Jerusalem and then moved into the regions of Judea and Samaria. Judea and Samaria were not the ends of the earth but they were also not the family and friends that lived in Jerusalem. Getting the message of Jesus to these places took some intentional effort. It meant being willing to go beyond their comfort zone and being willing to work with other believers to reach people in those areas.

Applying the meaning of Judea and Samaria to our modern day context is not an easy task. For the New Testament Church in Jerusalem reaching their Judea and Samaria clearly meant reaching people outside of their personal relationships and it meant working together to reach the local regions beyond Jerusalem.

In *Reaching Our World*, we see Judea and Samaria as representing local mission areas that are reached corporately alongside other believers. Can you think of any local missions efforts that your church is committed to reaching? _____

_____

_____

STEPS FOR REACHING YOUR JUDEA AND SAMARIA

The believers in Acts did not reach out to Judea and Samaria willingly. In fact, the Lord had to motivate them into obedience. What caused the spread of the gospel to Judea and Samaria according to Acts 8:1? _____

_____

What resulted in the scattering of believers due to persecution according to Acts 8:4? _____

_____

It would serve us well to preach the word of God to those people in our local areas before God has to force

WEEKLY BIBLE READING

Read the passage and write out an insight on at least one of the following:

A: Attitude to change
C: Command to obey
T: Truth to believe
S: Sin to confess

☐ **MONDAY**
Matthew 9:37-38

us there.

Imagine what would happen if everyone in your church shared a willing commitment to reach your Judea and Samaria. The message of Jesus would spread and more people would come to faith in Jesus. How was the spread of the gospel described in Acts 8:25? _____

_____

_____

_____

STEP ONE: IDENTIFY THE NEEDS

Reaching your local Judea and Samaria begins by identifying where the needs are. In every community, there are places where God's church can extend beyond it's own walls and reach people with the gospel. Identifying those needs will look very different in every church context but here are some examples of what those needs might look like.

A local food bank or homeless shelter
A crisis pregnancy center
A children's home or orphanage
A nursing home
An abused women's shelter

Not only should you look for places where needs exist, you should also look for people that have needs. In every community there are groups of people that have needs that the church can help meet. Together a church can have a serious impact on the world around them. Here are some examples of needs you might discover.

Single moms
Disabled Veteran's
Members of Law Enforcement or Firefighters
Prison Ministry
Cancer victims

STEP TWO: PRAY FOR GOD'S GUIDANCE

Imagine what might happen if every small group, ministry team, or Sunday School class in your church committed to praying for an area of local missions in your Judea and Samaria. What if every group in your church asked God to guide them to a local missions opportunity that crossed racial, economic, or social boundaries? What a powerful impact a church could have if every group or team was willing to ask God to open up a door and show them where he would have them go. How did Philip end up sharing the scriptures with the Ethiopian in Acts 8:26?

❏ **THURSDAY**
2 Corinthians
5:16-21

_____

_____

_____

What happened in Acts 8:29? _____

_____

_____

How could your small group begin to seek God about reaching our world through local missions? _____

_____

_____

❏ **FRIDAY**
Matthew 5:15-16

STEP THREE: WORK AS A TEAM

Most churches can have a greater impact on local missions when they commit to work together as a team to meet those needs. One great example of this is a small group that has adopted a local food bank to serve at once a month. Another example is a ministry team that has adopted a local fire station where they encourage firefighters two to three times a year. Small groups or ministry teams can easily adopt a place or people group within the context of local missions that they can regularly assist.

When a small group, class, or team adopts a group and serve them on a regular basis, those acts of kindness open the door for the gospel. What does Romans 2:4 tell us that acts of kindness are able to lead to?

_____

_____

17

Write the names of two or three places where your team could reach out together as an expression of local missions? _____

_____

STEP FOUR: BUILD RELATIONSHIPS

Reaching our world always comes down to people reaching people with the message of Christ. Even when you serve with acts of kindness in local mission settings, you will want to look for individual's you can build relationships with.

Where was Jesus in John 4:4, 5? _____

_____

Who does Jesus initiate a conversation with according to John 4:7? _____

_____

Jesus crosses several serious boundaries as he initiates a conversation with this Samaritan woman at the well. Jesus reaches past social and cultural boundaries to reveal himself to this Samaritan woman. What was the result of this revelation according to John 4:39? _____

_____

This encounter between Jesus and the Samaritan woman reminds us that building relationships is the ultimate goal in reaching our world. Even when we go beyond our own comfort zones the key is to connect with people so we can communicate the message of Christ.

STEP FIVE: SHARE THE GOOD NEWS

When you participate in a local outreach effort with your church or small group, the ultimate objective is to help communicate the good news of Jesus Christ. The goal is not just to demonstrate "acts of kindness". The goal is to let those acts of kindness create opportunities for a message of salvation. In other words, if you give a man a cup of water but don't tell him about the Living Water you have done him and injustice. If you give a woman bread to eat but fail to share with her the Bread of Life you have not really been very kind at all.

Reaching our world is ultimately about sharing the good news of Jesus with a lost and dying world. That means starting with our friends and family and then moving across boundaries to share with those we do not yet know. What was being reported in Acts 11:1? _____

_____

_____

30 DAY ACCOUNTABILITY GUIDE

Section 2

CORPO-RATE (CHURCH) OUTREACH	Church or Group Outreach	Corporate Prayer Focus	
	1._____ 2._____	☐ Week One ☐ Week Two ☐ Week Three ☐ Week Four	☐ Invited ☐ Participated

QUESTIONS FOR GROUP DISCUSSION
OR PERSONAL REFLECTION

☞ Which phrase best describes your current level of involvement in local missions?
(Pretty Strong, Hit or Miss, Very Weak)

☞ Take a minute and look at the Reaching Our World 30 Day Accountability Guide and share a few places that would be part of your personal Judea and Samaria.

☞ What boundaries in your contemporary context would be similar to the Judean and Samaritan context for the early Christians?

☞ Can you share some examples of groups or teams that you know of that have worked together to reach out in local missions?

☞ Why do you think the Christians in Jerusalem were initially reluctant to reach out to the areas of Judea and Samaria?

☞ What parallels do you see between the First Century Church and today's church when it comes to having an Acts 1:8 focus?

☞ What would it take for your small group to adopt a local missions emphasis?

☞ Describe what it would look like if every group in this church adopted a local missions focus?

☞ Spend a few minutes praying that this lesson would become a reality in your group and church.

WEEK FOUR: COMMITTED TO GLOBAL EVANGELISM

Goal: Understand How to Reach Your Ends of the Earth

MEMORY VERSE

Mark 16:15

The phrase "ends of the earth" has probably been interpreted many different ways over the past two thousand plus years. The difference in interpretation has likely involved each generation's knowledge of global expansion. In other words, "ends of the earth" would be interpreted differently by a First Century Christian living in Jerusalem than a Twenty First Century Christian living in North America.

One thing that every generation of believers has had in common is that the "ends of the earth" means everybody on the planet. From the time Jesus spoke the words in Acts 1:8 until today, the command to reach the world has never been in question. God has called every believer to be committed to global evangelism. We have clearly been told to reach our world!

WEEKLY BIBLE READING

Read the passage and write out an insight on at least one of the following:

A: Attitude to change
C: Command to obey
T: Truth to believe
S: Sin to confess

☐ **MONDAY**
Acts 13:44-52

STEPS FOR REACHING YOUR ENDS OF THE EARTH

Contrary to what some people might think, God can use everyone in global outreach. Being committed to global outreach does not mean you have to leave where you live. Global outreach might involve you moving to a different country but that would not be the case for the majority of Christians committed to reaching their ends of the earth. You can be an active part of reaching our world by praying, giving, encouraging, and supporting global outreach efforts done by individuals, churches, and mission ministries. It is just not that hard to be involved in global missions. It just takes a commitment on your part. List some missionaries or mission ministries with which you are familiar.

Why is global outreach so important according to John 3:16?

_____
_____

STEP ONE: LISTEN TO THE HOLY SPIRIT

The world is a pretty big place and discovering where God wants you to be involved in global outreach could be difficult to figure out. This is why you begin reaching the ends of the earth with prayer. What was taking place in the Church at Antioch in Acts 13:1-4? _____

_____
_____
_____

The Church was worshipping and seeking God when the Holy Spirit led them to send out Barnabas and Saul (Paul) to take the message outside of Jerusalem, Judea, and Samaria. This leading of the Holy Spirit became known as the first missionary journey of Paul. The first missionaries went where God was leading them and that strategy has not changed in over two thousand years. We should go wherever God leads!

STEP TWO: GO SHORT-TERM OR LONG-TERM

Sometimes God calls people to become lifetime missionaries and sometimes he just calls people to go somewhere for a week or two. Where did Paul and Barnabas go according to Acts 13:4? _____

_____
Where did they go according to Acts 13:13? _____

_____
Where did Paul end up according to Acts 14:6? ____

_____

Paul ended up going on three different mission trips that would be considered by many people in those days to be the "ends of the earth" to. In fact, notice how Paul describes his travels in Romans 15:19-21. How far did Paul travel? _____

_____

Paul did several short-term mission trips. He stayed more than a few weeks but he also went to more than one location over a period of time. God still uses people to reach people all around the globe when people are willing to go where He leads.

STEP THREE: PLANT CHURCHES

The Biblical model of missions is church planting. Can you name some of the churches Paul started or assisted on his journeys? _____

_____

_____

Who was with Paul according to Acts 18:18?_____

_____

Where did Paul meet Aquila and Priscilla according to Acts 18:1? _____

_____

What was going on in Aquila and Priscilla's house according to 1 Corinthians 16:19? _____

_____

Paul's mission trips involved traveling to places, meeting people, and starting churches. Paul often took return trips to make sure the churches he started were going strong.

STEP FOUR: SUPPORT MISSION EFFORTS

One very important way to participate in global missions is through giving and supporting missionaries and mission ministries. What had the believers in Corinth promised to do according to 1 Corinthians 9:5?_____

_____

☐ **THURSDAY**
Psalm 96:1-6

☐ **FRIDAY**
Matthew 28:16-20

What did Paul say about the church in Philippi according to Philippians 4:14-19? _____
_____
_____
_____

For well over two thousand years, the Church and Christians have been the primary means of supporting global outreach. It takes the generous gifts and resources of believers and churches to help get the gospel to the ends of the earth.

Imagine how much more could happen if individual Christians and local churches gave to support the work of global missions. Supporting missionaries, church based missions, and mission ministries are an important part of accomplishing global outreach.

STEP FIVE: ADOPT OR SPONSOR

Two great ways to get involved with global outreach without ever leaving home are to adopt a missionary or sponsor a child with a Christian organization. A small group, a class, or an individual can adopt a missionary and be a tremendous source of encouragement to them. Missionaries that live on the foreign mission field are certainly in need of ongoing encouragement and prayer. Adopting one missionary may not seem like much but it can go a long way to someone who has given their life to reaching people in other parts of the world. Sending regular notes and gifts can play a huge part in reaching our world.

Sponsoring a child through a Christian mission agency or church is another great way to impact the world. As children are taught the gospel in schools and orphanages they grow up to become influencers within that country. Sometimes reaching a child in another country is one of the most strategic ways to eventually reach others in that country. It is not only a smart thing to do; it is what Jesus would have done. Have you or do you sponsor a child through a Christian agency or church? _____

_____

STEP SIX: TEACH AND TALK ABOUT MISSIONS

Most churches have some type of mission emphasis or training they do every year or in certain settings. Obviously, if you teach the Bible you are going to teach missions! However, sometimes it helps to have a concentrated focus given just to the purpose of teaching what the Bible shows us regarding the importance of reaching our world. In fact, the whole Book of Acts is the story of how Acts 1:8 was implemented. It is a book about missions!

If your church does not have a specific plan for teaching about missions, this *Reaching Our World* course is a great tool for promoting and training people in your church or small group to have an outreach focus.

30 DAY ACCOUNTABILITY GUIDE

Section 3

GLOBAL OUTREACH	People Group, Missionary, or Mission Opportunity 1._____ 2._____ 3._____	Global Prayer Focus ☐ Week One ☐ Week Two ☐ Week Three ☐ Week Four	☐ Encouraged ☐ Supported ☐ Participated

NEXT STEPS IN REACHING OUR WORLD

Most of the time we work through a booklet like this one and then place it on the shelf and never look at it again. That should not be what you do with *Reaching Our World.* As you have noticed in each weekly lesson there is 30-Day Accountability Guide designed for use every thirty days on an ongoing basis. You can copy the 30-Day Guide and use it every month. The point is to be held accountable on a month-to-month basis for being an Acts 1:8 Disciple.

A second next step for *Reaching Our World* is to talk about how you are doing with reaching out at least once a month in your small group. Hopefully your group has a *Reaching Our World* Champion that takes the responsibility of leading the accountability time and sharing with your group outreach efforts of your church and group. You might even be willing to serve as that Champion if your group does not have someone already. Let your group leader know if you are interested.

The last step in applying *Reaching Our World* is to revisit this course every 12 or 24 months. This is one of those courses that will never get old and re-discussing these questions will help keep you sharp in outreach and evangelism. Let this course be the beginning and not the end of a lifestyle of reaching our world.

QUESTIONS FOR GROUP DISCUSSION OR PERSONAL REFLECTION

➤ Which phrase best describes your current level of involvement in global missions? (Pretty Strong, Hit or Miss, Very Weak)

➤ Take a minute and look at the Reaching Our World 30 Day Accountability Guide and share a few people groups, missionaries, or mission opportunities that would be part of your personal Ends of the Earth.

➤ How would the "ends of the earth" be interpreted differently today than in the first century?

➤ Why do we tend to think global missions only happens when we actually "go" over seas? How can we change that misperception?

➤ Why do you think the biblical model of missions a church-planting model?

➤ Have you ever been on a mission trip and, if so, how did it impact your life?

➤ Have you ever sponsored a child or supported a missionary? Share your experience.

➤ What do you think could happen if we took the 30-Day Accountability Guide seriously and used it individually and as a group?

➤ What would happen if a church developed a culture of reaching out to their Jerusalem, Judea & Samaria, and the Ends of the Earth?

➤ Take a few minutes to pray that your group and church would develop a heart for Reaching Our World.

A FEW FINAL THOUGHTS

Congratulations! You have finished *Reaching Our World*. Hopefully, you have applied yourself wholeheartedly to this study and are growing as a disciple of Christ.

Now that you know Christ's model for reaching out, I hope that you will make these principles an regular part of how you live. If you continue to apply these principles and live by these truths, you will grow closer to God, become more like Christ, and make an impact on the world.

It is time now to take your next step as a disciple and work through another course in the Disciple Making Extras Series. You may also want to check out more resources from Impact Ministries. Check out the Impact Ministries page in the back of this booklet or look us up on the web at ImpactDisciples.com.

Name:_____

_____ / **30 DAY ACCOUNTABILITY GUIDE** / Month:_____

COMMIT-MENTS	RECOGNIZE	PRAYER	ACTION
PERSONAL OUTREACH	Person or Place for Outreach 1._____ 2._____ 3._____	Personal Prayer Focus □ Week One □ Week Two □ Week Three □ Week Four	□ Invite □ Care / Serve □ Share
CORPO-RATE (CHURCH) OUTREACH	Church or Group Outreach 1._____ 2._____	Corporate Prayer Focus □ Week One □ Week Two □ Week Three □ Week Four	□ Invited □ Participated
GLOBAL OUTREACH	People Group, Missionary, or Mission Opportunity 1._____ 2._____ 3._____	Global Prayer Focus □ Week One □ Week Two □ Week Three □ Week Four	□ Encouraged □ Supported □ Participated

Inspiring People and Churches to Be and Build Disciples of Jesus Christ

EXPLORE

We invite you to EXPLORE and DISCOVER the concepts of DISCIPLE MAKING by checking out the following RESOURCES.

◆The Impact Blog ◆The Impact Newsletter
◆The Impact Audio and Video Podcasts

EDUCATE

We encourage you to LEARN more about DISCIPLE MAKING through our written RESOURCES and TRAINING opportunities.

◆The DMC Training ◆315 Leadership Training ◆Free Resources

ESTABLISH

We seek to HELP you start a DISCIPLE MAKING MOVEMENT by showing you how to LAUNCH a disciple making group.

◆The Impact Weekend ◆The Essentials ◆Vision Consultation

ENGAGE

We invite you to JOIN with Impact Ministries in spreading the VISION of DISCIPLE MAKING around the WORLD through several involvement opportunities.

◆Join our Prayer Team ◆Be an Impact Trainer ◆Partner with Us

CONTACT US

◆ImpactDisciples.com ◆Info@ImpactDisciples.com ◆678.854.9322

Made in the USA
Middletown, DE
16 May 2022

65816496R00022